STANDARD SUBMARINE PHRASEOLOGY

By Commander Submarines,
Atlantic fleet
United States navy

THIS TEXT HAS BEEN DIGITALLY WATERMARKED TO PREVENT ILLEGAL DUPLICATION.

ISBN #978-1-935700-51-7
©2008-2011 Periscope Film LLC
All Rights Reserved
www.PeriscopeFilm.com

STANDARD SUBMARINE PHRASEOLOGY

RESTRICTED

ISSUED BY
COMMANDER SUBMARINES, ATLANTIC FLEET

SECURITY NOTICE

This document contains information affecting the national defense of the United States within the meaning of the Espionage Act, 50 U.S.C., 31 and 32 as amended. Its transmission or the revelation of its contents in any manner to an unauthorized person is prohibited by law. ARTS. 75½ & 76, U.S.N. REGS., 1920.

The information contained in restricted documents and the essential characteristics of restricted material will not be communicated to the public or to the press, but may be given to any person known to be in the service of the United States and to persons of undoubted loyalty and discretion who are cooperating in Government work.

INTRODUCTION

The voice procedures and phraseology described in this booklet are recommended as standard for all submarine interior communications. These forms have been developed through the cooperative efforts of officers throughout the submarine fleet.

The general rules for formulating messages are given in the first section. The specific forms of phraseology to be used in various operations are covered in the succeeding sections. The communication circuit over which each message normally passes is stated, except for those messages which are directly airborne.

This booklet should be supplemented by a careful study of the SUBMARINE TELEPHONE TALKERS' MANUAL, which tells how to use the different types of communication equipment, and how to make a message understood in spite of interfering noise.

The use of *uniform* voice procedures and phraseology throughout the submarine fleet will save time, prevent confusion and mistakes, and increase the general efficiency of voice communications.

CONTENTS

VOICE PROCEDURES.........................	1
BATTLE STATIONS GUN ACTION............	7
BATTLE STATIONS TORPEDO................	8
CRUISING SUBMERGED	10
CRUISING SURFACED.........................	11
DIVING	12
EMERGENCY MESSAGES......................	14
ENGINE AND BATTERY COMBINATIONS....	15
GETTING UNDERWAY........................	16
LOOKOUTS...................................	17
RADAR.......................................	19
SONAR.......................................	22
SURFACING..................................	24

VOICE PROCEDURES

1. Components of a message

The typical message on a submarine consists of call and text. The call is the name of the station being addressed. The text is the body of the message. For example:

After room, open the outer doors.
 (call) (text)

In the rare cases when the source of a message is not obvious from the text, the identifying name of the sending station should be inserted following the call. For example: "Control, forward room, we heard a bumping noise along the hull."

The call is normally used because it serves the double purpose of alerting the correct listener and of helping to define the contents of the message. It should be omitted only when speed is essential and when the text of the message clearly indicates to whom it is addressed. For example: "Rig for depth charge."

2. Acknowledgments

Every message is acknowledged, but the method of acknowledgment varies with the type of message, as follows:

(a) Orders

Orders addressed to an individual or to a single compartment are acknowledged by repeating them back word for word. This repetition serves as a check on the accuracy of the reception of the order, and passes the word for action to other men in the compartment.

(Order) **Forward room, set depth one ze-ro feet.**

(Acknowledgment) **Forward room, set depth one ze-ro feet.**

Orders addressed to all compartments are acknowledged from forward aft by giving the name of the compartment and adding "aye".

(Order) **All compartments, secure from depth charge.**

(Acknowledgment) **Forward room, aye.**

Battery forward, aye. Etc.

RESTRICTED

(b) Reports

When the correct reception of its details is important, the report is repeated back word for word.

 (Report)   JP, contact, bearing two one ze-ro.

(Acknowledgment) JP, contact, bearing two one ze-ro.

When a report of a routine nature is heard directly by the person to whom it is addressed, "Very well" or "Aye, aye" is usually sufficient acknowledgment.

(c) Questions

When a question can be answered immediately, the answer in itself constitutes an acknowledgement. The answer should be worded so that it is clear that the question has been understood.

 (Question) Forward room, how are your bilges?

 (Answer)   Control, forward room bilges are dry.

When a question cannot be answered immediately, the immediate acknowledgment is normally a repetition of the question and the word, "Wait". For questions of a routine nature, "Aye, aye," plus "Wait" is usually sufficient acknowledgment. In either case, the answer is given as soon as the information becomes available.

 (Question) Forward room, how are your bilges?

(Acknowledgment) Forward room, how are your bilges? Wait.

 (Answer)   Control, six inches of water in forward room bilges.

3. Correction or change in a message

If the sender makes a mistake in giving a message, he says "Belay that" and gives the correct form.

  Gyros forward, set gyros by hand ze-ro ze-ro fo-wer. Belay that.

  Set gyros by hand ze-ro fo-wer fo-wer.

If the receiving station repeats a message incorrectly, the sender says "Belay that" and gives the correct message again.

RESTRICTED

4. Reports of execution

When an order has been carried out, this fact is reported to the station originating the order. Generally, the report of execution closely follows the wording of the order.

(Order)	After room, open the outer doors.
(Acknowledgment)	After room, open the outer doors.
(Report)	Conning tower, the outer doors have been opened aft.

Other common forms in reports of execution involve the phrases "has the word" and "on his way."

(Order)	Tell Mr. R. to check the gun access hatch.
(Report)	Mr. R. has the word.
(Order)	Gunner's mate to the bridge.
(Report)	The gunner's mate is on his way.

Certain special forms are given later in this manual.

5. Request for a repeat

If the receiver fails to understand any part of a message, he says "Repeat". The sender then gives the entire message again.

(Message)	JP, pick up target bearing wuh wuh nay.
(Reply)	Repeat.
(Message)	JP, pick up target bearing one one eight.

6. Emergency messages

In case of an emergency, the station making the announcement calls:

Silence on the line.

All other stations cease talking immediately until the word "Carry on" is received. If any message was interrupted by the emergency announcement, it is then repeated in full.

7. Station tests

A station test is conducted whenever a circuit is newly-manned, or when there is some question whether particular stations have been manned, and also at hourly intervals during each watch. The nature of the test is indicated by the following example:

    (Order)   **All compartments, control testing.**

    (Reports)   **Forward room, aye.**

                        Battery forward, aye.

                        Conning tower, aye. Etc.

The stations answer in order from forward aft. If any station does not reply within five seconds, the next station comes in. The station passed over then enters at the end of the list.

Below are the correct station names on communication circuits. These particular names have been selected on the basis of tests which showed them to be the most easily understood and the least readily confused.

Forward room	Gyros forward
Battery forward	Gyros aft
Control	TDC
Conning tower	Bridge
Battery aft	Forward capstan
Forward engine room	After capstan
After engine room	Deck gun
Maneuvering	JP
After room	

8. Shifting phones

A change of talkers at a telephone station during a watch is reported to the control station by the talker being relieved. The change of phones is made as soon as the report has been acknowledged. The new talker then reports his presence on the line. The control station may be either the control room or the conning tower.

    (Report)   **Control, forward room shifting phones.**

    (Acknowledgment) **Control, forward room shifting phones.**

    (Report)   **Control, forward room back on the line.**

9. Securing phones

Typically, phones are secured on receipt of an order from the control station.

    (Order)   **All compartments, secure phones.**

    (Reports)   **Forward room, securing phones.**

                     Battery forward, securing phones. Etc.

Phones are never secured without permission from the OOD. In special instances, it may be necessary to ask permission to secure.

        Control, permission to secure phones in battery aft.

After the permission is granted, the station reports that it is securing.

10. Frequently-used terms

The following terms, which are common to a number of commands, are used to avoid confusion and misunderstanding.

(a)   'Section one,' 'Section two,' and 'Section thuh-ree.'

      'First section' sounds too much like 'third section'.

(b)   'Shut.'

      'Close' is often mistaken for 'open' or 'blow'.

(c)   'Shoot' in preliminary commands.

      'Fire' is used only when giving orders to open fire.

(d)   'Permission to ...' as a standard request before beginning an operation requiring special permission. For example: "Permission to start an air charge." "Granted."

(e)   'Man' and 'secure', as applied to various types of equipment.

RESTRICTED

11. Numerals in messages

The pronunciation of numerals as shown at the right is now standard for all the services. The numeral '0' is spoken as 'ze-ro' except in giving ranges. For ranges, it is called "oh". When '00' occurs at the end of a range, it is called 'double-oh'. '000' at the end of a range is called 'oh double-oh'. '0000' at the end of a range is called 'oh oh double-oh'. Other rules for the use of numbers in messages are as follows:

ZE-RO
WUN
TOO
THUH-REE
FO-WER
FI-YIV
SIX
SEVEN
ATE
NINER

(a) Courses and bearings are spoken as three separate digits. (All bearings are understood to be relative unless followed by the word 'true'.)

Steer course two fi-yiv fo-wer.

Bearing ze-ro ze-ro six.

Bearing one fi-yiv fo-wer, TRUE.

(b) Speed, depth to keel, and torpedo depth are spoken as two separate digits.

Speed ze-ro six knots.

Six fi-yiv feet.

Set depth at one two feet.

(c) Angle-on-the-bow is spoken as an ordinary compound number, preceded by 'port' or 'starboard'.

Angle-on-the-bow, port thirty fi-yiv.

(d) Angle of the boat and planes are spoken as ordinary compound numbers.

Two degree up angle, twenty degree rise on the bow planes.

(e) Time is given in standard Navy terminology.

Ze-ro ze-ro thirty.

Seventeen thirty fi-yiv.

Ze-ro eight hundred.

12. Brevity

Messages are given in standard form whenever possible, and are always kept brief. Words like 'please', 'sir', and 'thank you' are not used on interior communication circuits.

BATTLE STATIONS GUN ACTION

Typical orders used in battle stations gun action are given below. The detailed content of some of these will vary with the circumstances, but the general phrasing should remain the same.

From	Over	Orders
CO	1MC	Battle stations gun action. Deck gun only.
Gunnery officer	XJA	Battery aft, fill the ammunition train.
		When ammunition train is filled, battery aft reports this fact to the gunnery officer.
Gunnery officer	7MC	Gunnery officer ready.
CO	7MC	Target is small sampan, bearing one two ze-ro, range fi-yiv oh double-oh.
CO	7MC	Stand by for battle surface.
		For surfacing phraseology see page 24.
CO	7MC	Open gun access hatch. Gun crew on deck.
CO	1JP	Deck gun commence firing.
Gun captain		Ready one. Fire one. Check fire.
		Range fo-wer six double-oh. Scale fi-yiv eight. Resume fire.
		In an emergency any man may call: "Silence!" After the emergency is over the gun captain says: "Carry on."
CO	1JP	Cease firing. Secure the deck gun. Clear the deck.
		Last man down reports: "Gun access door shut."
CO	1MC	Secure from battle stations.

RESTRICTED

BATTLE STATIONS TORPEDO

The phraseology for battle stations torpedo is the same, whether the submarine is submerged or surfaced. For clarity, the following examples are arranged in three divisions according to the units receiving the orders.

To all compartments over 1MC

Battle stations torpedo.

> XJA and JA talkers in conning tower conduct a station test.

Tracking party, man your stations.

> This order is used as an alternative to the first when it is desired to track the target without manning all battle stations. Communication among members of the tracking party takes place over 7MC, plus any auxiliary circuits which have been set up linking conning tower, plot, radar, and sonar.

Rig for depth charge. (Over XJA)

> When all compartments have reported rigged for depth charge, the conning tower talker reports this fact.

Secure from battle stations. Section one take the watch.

To gyro regulators over JA

Gyros forward, match gyros by hand.

Gyros aft, shift to automatic.

Gyros forward, stand by to check gyros ... Mark!

> Reports from gyros forward would be:
>
> > Standing by ... Thuh-ree fo-wer ze-ro.

Gyros forward, shift to hand. (in case of casualty)

Gyros forward, set gyros on thuh-ree fi-yiv six.

To torpedo talkers over XJA

Forward room, order of tubes is one, two, thuh-ree, fo-wer.

Forward room, make ready the forward tubes.

After room, except for opening the outer doors, make ready the after tubes.

Forward room, set depth ze-ro eight feet.

After room, open the outer doors on tubes seven and eight.

Forward room, stand by. Fire one. Fire two. Fire thuh-ree.

> After receiving the report from the forward room that these tubes have been fired, the conning tower talker reports this fact to the approach officer.

Reload tubes one, two, thuh-ree.

> This order is followed by a series of reports:
>
> > Conning tower, commencing reload forward.
> >
> > Conning tower, torpedo entering number one tube.
> >
> > Conning tower, reload completed on number one tube.
>
> When all designated tubes have been reloaded:
>
> > Conning tower, reload completed forward.

After room, secure the after tubes.

For emergency firing

Emergency torpedoes forward.

> When outer doors are open, forward room reports:
>
> > Conning tower, tubes one, two ready.

Fire one. Fire two.

CRUISING SUBMERGED

Below are typical examples of orders used in normal submerged cruising. All come from the conning tower over XJA.

Rig for silent running.

> When all compartments have reported rigged for silent running, the conning tower talker reports this fact. All communication during silent running is over the XJA circuit.

Secure from silent running.

Report leaks.

After room, load a red smoke.

After room, fire a red smoke.

Forward room, lower the port sound-head.

Forward room, shift to hand-training on the starboard sound-head.

> This order is used only in case of casualty to the remote-control training mechanism.

CRUISING SURFACED

These examples cover the miscellaneous orders used in the general operation of the ship. Bridge orders over XJA are usually relayed by the conning tower.

From	Over	Orders and reports
Bridge	XJA	Forward room, rig out the bendix (pit) log.
Control	7MC	Bridge, permission to test the bow planes.
Bridge	7MC	Control, cut in the bridge gyro-repeater and the bridge rudder-angle indicator.
Conning tower	7MC	Control, notify the Captain we changed course to one eight ze-ro at twenty-one nineteen, when log read seven two and a half.
Bridge	XJA	Maneuvering, start a battery charge on two main engines. Maneuvering acknowledges by stating which engines are being used.
Bridge	XJA	Maneuvering, carry a one hundred amp float with thuh-ree generators.
Bridge	XJA	Maneuvering, get a gravity reading. A typical report would be: "Conning tower, gravity forward twelve fifty, temperature one eighteen. Gravity aft twelve forty-eight, temperature one fourteen."
Bridge	7MC	Control, darken the control room.
Bridge	7MC	Control, dump garbage through the conning tower hatch.
Bridge	7MC	Control, blow all sanitary tanks.
Bridge	XJA	Forward engine room, how are your bilges?
Control	7MC	Bridge, keep clear of antenna. We are transmitting.
Bridge	XJA	Battery aft, gunner's mate to the bridge.
Bridge or conning tower	7MC	Control, reading on the DRAI. A typical report would be: "DRAI reading, thirty-eight degrees twenty-five minutes north, one hundred sixty-one degrees six minutes east."

RESTRICTED

DIVING

Examples of messages to and from the CO or OOD are given first. The basic diving orders and reports have been starred (*). Other messages are often omitted, except during training dives or under other special circumstances. Examples of orders from the diving officer are divided according to the units receiving them.

From	*Over*	*Orders and reports*
Bridge	1MC	*Rig for dive. When all compartments have reported that they are rigged for dive, control room reports this fact to the bridge.
Bridge	7MC	Have Mr. R. check the gun access hatch.
CO		Clear the bridge.
CO or OOD	1MC	*Dive, dive, dive. At the same time, the diving alarm is sounded.
Diving officer		*Pressure in the boat, green board.
CO	7MC	*Six fi-yiv feet.
Diving officer	XJA	*Open bulkhead flappers and start the ventilation. All compartments report in turn that bulkhead flappers are open. The forward engine room also reports ventilation started.
Diving officer		One-third trim, niner ze-ro feet, two degree up bubble.
Diving officer		*Final trim, six fi-yiv feet.
Diving officer		Request speed.
CO	7MC	Take her down. (*for deep dives*)

RESTRICTED

Orders from Diving Officer to Control Room

To hydraulic manifold:

Open all main vents. Vent negative. Cycle the vents.

Flood safety. Flood negative. Shut the negative flood.

To trim manifold:

Pump from forward trim to after trim.
Air manifold reports: "Suction on forward trim, after trim venting."

Pump from auxiliary to sea. Flood auxiliary from sea.

Pump from auxiliary to after trim, fi-yiv hundred pounds.

Pump from forward trim to auxiliary, and report every fi-yiv hundred pounds.
Trim manifold reports: "Fi-yiv hundred out." "One thousand out." Etc.

To air manifold:

Bleed air.

Blow all main ballast tanks. Blow negative.

Secure the air.

To planesmen:

Niner ze-ro feet. Six fi-yiv feet.

Two degrees up bubble. Thuh-ree degrees down bubble.

Ease the bubble. Ze-ro bubble.

Twenty degree rise on the bow planes. Ten degrees dive on the stern planes.

Take charge of your planes.

Orders from Diving Officer over XJA

Forward room, shift bow buoyancy vent to hand.

Forward room, open bow buoyancy vent by hand.

After room, shut number seven main ballast vent by hand.

Forward engine room, open number fi-yiv fuel ballast flood valves by hand.

RESTRICTED

EMERGENCY MESSAGES

The examples below show a typical series of emergency messages concerned with a fire discovered in battery aft. The same forms are used for other emergencies such as chlorine and collision.

From	Over	Orders and reports
Battery aft	XJA	Silence on the line. Fire in battery aft.
Control	1MC	Fire in battery aft.
		All stations immediately rig for fire, then report in turn from forward aft.
Control	XJA	Battery aft, open battery-disconnect switches.
Battery aft	XJA	Control, fire checked in battery aft.
Battery aft	XJA	Control, fire stopped in battery aft.
Control	1MC	All compartments, secure from fire.

ENGINE AND BATTERY COMBINATIONS

Unless the bridge has a talker on the XJA circuit, these messages are usually relayed from the bridge to the maneuvering room by the XJA conning tower talker. Normally, the bridge specifies only the number of engines to be used in propulsion or charging. In acknowledging the order, the maneuvering room states exactly which engines are being used. This is illustrated in the first example below.

Answer bells on two main engines.

> Report from maneuvering room:
>
> **Answering bells on one and two main engines.**

All ahead one-third.

> After the maneuvering room has answered the annunciator, the conning tower talker reports:
>
> **All answer ahead one-third.**

Port back two-thirds.

> The conning tower talker reports:
>
> **Port answers back two-thirds.**

Answer bells on thuh-ree main engines. Put one main engine on charge.

Standard speed will be one eight knots.

Make seven fi-yiv turns.

Make turns for one fo-wer knots.

Answer bells on battery. Secure the engines.

GETTING UNDERWAY

Orders for line-handling, to the anchor detail, and to the helm are given in standard Navy language. These are omitted here.

From	Over	Orders
Bridge	1MC	Make all preparations for getting underway.
Bridge	1MC	Station the maneuvering watch.
		When all stations have reported that they are manned, the bridge talker reports to the CO: **All stations ready to get underway; maneuvering watch set.**
Conning tower	XJA	Maneuvering, test your annunciators.
Conning tower	XJA	Maneuvering, answer bells on the engines.
Conning tower	XJA	After room and Control, stand by to check the steering.
Bridge	1MC	Rig for dive.
Bridge	1MC	Station the regular sea detail: section one.

LOOKOUTS

The three basic lookouts are known as "Port Lookout," "Starboard Lookout," and "Stern Lookout." If additional lookouts are used, they should be given call names appropriate to their functions on the bridge.

Stationing the lookout watch

OOD to CPO of the watch:	Assemble the lookouts.
CPO of the watch to OOD:	Lookouts in the control room.
OOD:	Lookouts to the bridge.

Relieving a lookout

Relief lookout to OOD:	Permission to relieve port lookout.
OOD:	Granted.
Relief to duty lookout:	Ready.
Duty lookout to relief:	Your sector is two four ze-ro to ze-ro ze-ro ze-ro. Sector clear. (or) Ship, two eight ze-ro, horizon, has been reported.
Duty lookout to OOD:	Port lookout relieved.

Search orders from OOD

Starboard lookout, search from ze-ro fi-yiv ze-ro to ze-ro seven ze-ro.

Stern lookout, remain on target.

Starboard lookout, resume sector search.

Clearing the bridge

Lookouts below. (or) **Clear the bridge.**

> *This normally precedes an order to dive.*

(See next page for reports by lookouts)

RESTRICTED

Reports by Lookouts

1. Surface objects.

    (a) Nature of the object: ship, periscope, light, rocket, flare, smoke, land, buoy, bubble, torpedo wake, oil slick, etc.
    If uncertain, simply say 'object.'

    (b) Relative bearing in three digits.

    (c) Approximate range: horizon, halfway, or close aboard.
    If ship doctrine calls for closer estimation, give range in thousands of yards.

    Ship, two ze-ro fi-yiv, horizon.

    Land, one eight fi-yiv, ten thousand yards.

2. Distant aircraft.

    (a) The words 'plane' and 'far'.

    (b) Relative bearing in three digits.

    (c) Elevation.

    (d) Approximate course of plane: approaching, parallel course, crossing bow, crossing stern.

    Plane, far, one one ze-ro, elevation fo-wer, approaching.

3. Nearby aircraft.

    (a) The word 'plane'.

    (b) The word 'close'.

    Plane, close.

Note: At the conclusion of the initial search upon taking over a watch, the lookout reports his sector clear if nothing is sighted.

   Port clear. (or) **Stern clear.** (or) **Starboard clear.**

RADAR

Orders begin with RADAR for the station in the conning tower, or with SUGAR DOG for the station in the control room.

Reports typically begin with the name of the radar station or the specific radar equipment from which the reports originate. The radar equipment should be referred to as follows:

SUGAR DOG	APR
SUGAR JIG	BK
SUGAR TARE	BN

When a rapid series of reports is coming from a radar operator, the conning tower may direct the operator to omit this identification. The identification is always omitted in reporting plane contacts because it is understood that all plane reports come from Sugar Dog.

Initial contacts — Upon making a contact, the Sugar Jig operator immediately reports contact, bearing, and range. The Sugar Dog operator immediately reports contact and range. As soon as possible, he adds whether the target is opening, closing, or standing still.

Supplementary reports — Without further orders, radar operators report all additional information as soon as it is observed. This includes:

1. Identification and further details concerning targets, such as size of ship, number of planes, etc.
2. Revised judgment as to identification, size, number, etc.
3. Marked changes in target, such as change in range rate.
4. Lost contact, giving range and bearing of last observed position.
5. Evidence of radar jamming, interference, or deception.
6. Failure or improper operation of equipment.

Sugar Jig and Sugar Tare

Orders	*Reports*
Radar, make a hand sweep on A-scope. Use mean scale.	Radar, all clear to .... thousand yards.
Radar, make an automatic sweep on PPI. Use .... thousand yard scale.	Radar, land contact, bearing from ze-ro two seven to one thuh-ree six, range

RESTRICTED

Sugar Jig and Sugar Tare (Continued)

Orders	*Reports*
Radar, search from one ze-ro ze-ro to one fi-yiv zero.	Radar, contact, bearing one fo-wer ze-ro, range .....
	Radar, doubtful contact, bearing one niner two, range .....
Radar tracking party, man your stations.	Radar tracking stations manned.
Radar, track target bearing two seven ze-ro, range	Radar, no contact bearing two seven ze-ro, range .....
Radar, shift to Sugar Tare.	Radar shifted to Sugar Tare.
Radar, mark the range.	Radar, stand by. Mark! Range .....
Radar, shift to Sugar Jig.	Radar shifted to Sugar Jig.
Radar, report bearings and ranges to Plot.	Radar, stand by. Mark! Bearing one one two. Range .....
Radar, make a PPI sweep and return to target.	Radar, two contacts. Bearing one one ze-ro. Range ..... Bearing one fi-yiv fo-wer. Range .....
Radar, get the bearing and range to nearest land.	Radar, land from bearing thuh-ree fo-wer fi-yiv to ze-ro two ze-ro. Nearest range .... on bearing ze-ro ze-ro fi-yiv.
	Radar contact lost, bearing two seven eight, range ..... Range too great.
	Radar reports jamming from bearing one one zero to one fo-wer fi-yiv.
	Sugar Jig is not operating properly.
Radar, put the Sugar Jig in stand-by condition.	Sugar Jig is in stand-by condition.

Sugar Dog

Orders	*Reports*
Sugar Dog, make a two-second search.	Sugar Dog, all clear.
	Plane contacts at .... and .... miles.
	Plane contact .... miles, large formation, closing fast.
	Plane contact lost at .... miles.
Sugar Dog, put the Sugar Dog in stand-by condition.	Sugar Dog is in stand-by condition.

IFF

Orders	*Reports*
Radar, challenge contact, bearing one one thuh-ree, range	Radar, contact, bearing one one thuh-ree, range ...., is friendly.
Sugar Dog, challenge contact, range	Sugar Dog, contact, range ...., does not reply.

APR

Orders	*Reports*
	APR contact, enemy (or friendly).
APR, describe enemy contact.	APR contact is .... megacyles.
	Pulse rate ..... Signal steady.
	Intensity moderate.

RESTRICTED

SONAR

Orders to sonar stations and reports from sonar stations begin with the station name. Station names are as follows:

    QB — for the QB operator
    JK — for the JK/QC operator, regardless of which gear he is using
    JP — for the JP operator

When communication from a sonar operator becomes continuous, as in giving a rapid series of bearings during an approach, the conning tower may direct the operator to omit this identification. Under the same circumstances, acknowledgments may also be omitted.

Sonar operators report all essential information as soon as it becomes available, using the standard forms of phraseology whenever possible.

Orders	*Reports*
JP, search from starboard beam to bow.	JP, clear all around.
QB, search thirty degrees on each side of the bow.	QB, contact, bearing ze-ro one fi-yiv.
	QB, doubtful contact, bearing thuh-ree fi-yiv ze-ro.
JP, pick up target bearing ze-ro eight six.	JP, target bearing ze-ro eight fo-wer, slow heavy screws.
QB, stay on target bearing two fo-wer seven.	QB, target bearing two fo-wer seven, light screws speeding up.
JP, shift to target bearing two one fi-yiv.	JP, target bearing two one fi-yiv drawing aft.
QB, report bearings every two degrees.	QB, lost contact, last bearing two fo-wer fi-yiv.
JP, give me a mark on bearing two one ze-ro.	JP, mark! Bearing two one ze-ro.
	JP, bearing two ze-ro niner. Turn count is ze-ro niner six.
JP, follow our torpedoes.	JP, torpedoes running at thuh-ree fo-wer fi-yiv and thuh-ree fo-wer niner.
JP, monitor ship's noise.	JP, high noise level bearing one six one. Sounds like generator.

Orders	*Reports*
QB, make a frequency sweep.	QB, contact, echo-ranging. Long scale. Still searching.
	QB, contact, echo-ranging. Short scale. Directly on us.
QB, get the frequency of echo-ranging.	QB, frequency of echo-ranging is ten kilocycles.
QB, get a single-ping range.	QB, range one oh fi-yiv oh. Good range.
	QB, no range.
QB, get true bearing of target.	QB, bearing one one seven, TRUE.
	JP operator relieved. Smith has the watch.

SURFACING

In these examples, the basic surfacing orders have been starred (*). Orders from the diving officer are similar to those used in diving, as given on page 13, and are therefore not repeated here.

From	Over	Orders and reports
Conning tower	1MC	*Make all preparations for surfacing.
Conning tower	XJA	*Maneuvering, on surfacing answer bells on thuh-ree main engines; put one main engine on charge.
Diving officer	XJA	*Secure the ventilation. Shut bulkhead flappers.
		All compartments report in turn that bulkhead flappers are shut. The forward engine room also reports ventilation secured.
Diving officer		*Ready to surface in all respects.
Conning tower	1MC	*Surface.
		The surfacing alarm is sounded at the same time. The diving officer gives the necessary orders to the manifolds.
CO		Open the hatch. Open the main induction.
CO		Lookouts to the bridge.
Diving officer		Low pressure blowers secured. Safety and negative flooded. Ready to dive.

This is one of five publications prepared by Commander Submarines, Atlantic Fleet, with the collaboration of officers throughout the submarine service. The National Defense Research Committee and the Medical Research Department, New London Submarine Base, assisted in research and in preparation of the manuscript.

The entire series includes:

1. *Submarine Telephone Talkers' Manual*
2. *Standard Submarine Phraseology*
3. *Ship's Organization Chapter on Voice Communications*
4. Phonograph Recording — *Telephone Talking over a Submarine Battle Circuit During Actual Operation* and *Analysis of Telephone Talking over a Submarine Battle Circuit*
5. *Instructors Handbook for Basic Course in Submarine Voice Communications*

Additional copies of the *Submarine Telephone Talkers' Manual*, NAVPERS 16171, should be requested from the Chief of Naval Personnel. Others in the series should be requested from Commander Submarines, Atlantic Fleet, Fleet Post Office, New York, N. Y.

ISBN #978-1-935700-51-7
©2008-2011 Periscope Film LLC
All Rights Reserved
www.PeriscopeFilm.com

www.ingramcontent.com/pod-product-compliance
Lightning Source LLC
Chambersburg PA
CBHW081356040426
42451CB00017B/3479